summersdale

Let the
FUN
be GIN

LET THE FUN BeGIN

An Hachette UK Company
www.hachette.co.uk

Summersdale Publishers Ltd
Part of Octopus Publishing Group Limited
Carmelite House
50 Victoria Embankment
LONDON
EC4Y 0DZ
UK

www.summersdale.com

Printed and bound in the Czech Republic

ISBN: 978-1-78685-768-2

Please drink responsibly

Substantial discounts on bulk quantities of Summersdale books are available to corporations, professional associations and other organisations. For details contact general enquiries: telephone: +44 (0) 1243 771107 or email: enquiries@summersdale.com.

TO ....

FROM ....

WHAT IS GIN?

Gin is a clear spirit that is distilled from grain or malt and flavoured with juniper. Juniper is the main component for making gin 'gin', as without it you'd just have flavoured vodka. It acts as the foundation, to which you add other botanicals in order to create a well-balanced aromatic flavour.

In a way, making gin is like making perfume and, like perfumes, each one is different. Some of the most popular gins on the market are:

London Dry gin – this is infused with botanicals during its second or third distillation process.

Plymouth gin – this has a similar production process to London Dry gin, although it uses different aromatic ingredients.

Old Tom gin – this was originally used in a Tom Collins cocktail and is a recipe that had almost fallen out of favour until the gin renaissance of recent years.

Dutch gin *(jenever)* – this is the original gin recipe, although it looks and tastes very different to the gin most people know and love today. Distilled from malt grains, it is more like whisky than other gins.

A DASH
OF HISTORY

Production of gin (*jenever*) began in Holland in the sixteenth century and it was first used as a medicinal drink to treat stomach aches, gout and gallstones.

During the Thirty Years' War, it made its way to the British troops fighting in the Low Countries. It was used to warm up the soldiers, who faced damp weather conditions, and also became the go-to drink when they needed a bit of 'Dutch courage'.

Gin was slowly introduced to England upon the soldiers' return to their home country and distillation of the spirit commenced, albeit without any of the health and safety regulations that have to be adhered to nowadays. It was the drink of choice for the poor and was blamed for crime, prostitution and mental illness until the Gin Act of September 1736 was introduced, which put a tax on gin and introduced a licence for gin sellers. This provoked riots and made the spirit unaffordable to most – only two distilleries ended up agreeing to the terms of the licence. Seven years later, the act was repealed and a new policy was drafted that set lower taxes, benefitting a bigger variety of good-quality distillers and retailers alike.

GIN FOR

If you haven't noticed already, gin is everywhere. In some pubs and restaurants they are even advertising it as a substitute for soup! In trendy bars, just take one glance and you'll notice hipsters supping the gin cocktail special while connoisseurs are testing the latest botanical flavours.

Distilleries have been experimenting with new tastes and combinations to create exciting new gin flavours. Gin bars have also seen a rise in popularity, with mixologists recreating classic cocktails and inventing new and exclusive recipes of their own. With so many flavours to try, no wonder the gin boom has got everyone talking.

EVERYONE

KNOWING YOUR BOTANICALS

There are many botanicals used in flavouring gin. Here are some of the most common ones:

Juniper – if a gin distillery doesn't use this coniferous plant in their production process then they can't promote their gin as distilled. It gives the gin a citrus taste, which can be enhanced with...

Lemon and orange peel – these peels can be used together or separately in order to flavour gin. You can adjust the sweetness or bitterness of the flavour by changing the variety of fruit you use.

Coriander – often considered the second most important botanical in gin, coriander seeds are used to add a touch of spice and fragrance to the mix.

Angelica root – another warming flavour and one of the nine traditional ingredients in gin-making.

Orris root – this is the bulb of the iris plant. It is bitter and takes up to four years to mature enough for use.

Liquorice, cassia bark and nutmeg – these, along with the previous six ingredients, comprise the nine traditional gin botanicals. Other modern, popular flavourings include ginger, cubeb berries, cardamom, almond, cinnamon, angelica seeds and camomile flowers.

WHAT YOU NEED

In order to make the gin recipes in this book, you will find the following equipment useful:

A cocktail shaker – if you can find one that has a built-in strainer it will help you when you come to pour the cocktails. Alternatively, you can use a tea strainer.

A variety of different glasses – depending on the type of cocktail you're making, you will need an assortment of small and large glasses. Champagne flutes and cocktail, Old-fashioned, Collins, coupe, Sling, Martini, Copa de Balon and highball glasses are the most commonly used.

Bar spoon – if you don't have one of these to hand, use a chopstick for when you need to stir a cocktail.

Lemon and lime squeezer – this is a useful piece of equipment to separate the pips from your freshly squeezed juice. Alternatively, you could use your fingers and pick out the pips.

Ice – you'll need cubes of ice for most recipes, but some require crushed ice, where stated.

Sugar syrup – you can make this easily at home and it lasts up to six months if refrigerated. Add one part water and two parts caster sugar to a saucepan and brIng to the boil. Turn the heat to low and stir constantly until the sugar has completely dissolved. Allow the syrup to cool and then pour into a sterilised jar and seal with a lid.

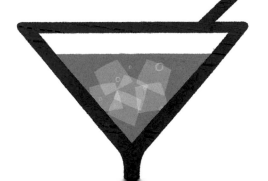

THE ONLY TIME
I EVER ENJOYED
IRONING WAS THE
DAY I ACCIDENTALLY
GOT GIN IN THE
STEAM IRON.

PHYLLIS DILLER

WHEN YOU STOP
DRINKING,
YOU HAVE TO
DEAL WITH THIS
MARVELLOUS
PERSONALITY
THAT STARTED YOU
DRINKING IN THE
FIRST PLACE.

JIMMY BRESLIN

I'M NOT A HEAVY DRINKER;
I CAN SOMETIMES GO FOR
HOURS WITHOUT
TOUCHING A
DROP.

NOËL COWARD

GIN FIZZ

This long-standing classic and New Orleans favourite was invented in 1888 by Henry C. Ramos in the Imperial Cabinet Saloon, New Orleans.

INGREDIENTS

60 ml gin · 1 tsp sugar or sugar syrup
Dash of freshly squeezed lemon juice
Soda water to finish · Slice of lemon
to garnish · 1 egg white (optional)

METHOD

In a cocktail shaker filled with ice, mix together the gin, lemon juice, sugar or syrup and egg white. Shake vigorously and strain into a highball glass.

Fill to the top with soda water and serve with a slice of lemon.

I'M A DRINKER

WITH WRITING
PROBLEMS.

BRENDAN
BEHAN

WHEN YOU'RE
THIRSTY AND IT
SEEMS THAT YOU
COULD DRINK THE
ENTIRE OCEAN,
THAT'S FAITH;
WHEN YOU START
TO DRINK AND
FINISH ONLY A
GLASS OR TWO,
THAT'S SCIENCE.

ANTON CHEKHOV

I distrust camels, and anyone else who can go a week without a drink.

Joe E. Lewis

BRAMBLE

Dick Bradsell, the legendary London bartender and inventor of the Bramble, also created other classics such as the Espresso Martini and Russian Spring Punch.

INGREDIENTS

60 ml gin · 30 ml freshly squeezed lemon juice · 15 ml sugar syrup · 15 ml crème de mûre · Blackberries to garnish

METHOD

Fill an Old-fashioned glass with crushed ice and add the gin, lemon juice and sugar syrup.

Top with more crushed ice and pour the crème de mûre over the top. Garnish with a couple of blackberries.

I EXERCISE STRONG
SELF-CONTROL.
I NEVER DRINK
ANYTHING STRONGER
THAN GIN BEFORE
BREAKFAST.

W. C. FIELDS

IGNORANCE
IS A LOT LIKE
ALCOHOL:
THE MORE YOU
HAVE OF IT,
THE LESS YOU ARE
ABLE TO SEE ITS
EFFECT ON YOU.

JAY M. BYLSMA

I THINK THAT
I WILL TAKE TWO
SMALL BOTTLES
OF DUBONNET
AND GIN WITH ME
THIS MORNING,
IN CASE IT
IS NEEDED.

THE QUEEN MOTHER

GIMLET

The original recipe quantities recorded in *The Savoy Cocktail Book* are half gin and half Rose's lime juice, but modern tastes have changed and so has the recipe.

INGREDIENTS

60 ml gin · 15 ml Rose's lime juice
Slice of lime to garnish

METHOD

Shake together in a cocktail shaker with ice and strain into a cocktail glass. Garnish with a slice of lime.

A REAL GIMLET IS
HALF GIN AND HALF
ROSE'S LIME JUICE
AND NOTHING ELSE.

RAYMOND CHANDLER

EAT.
SLEEP.
GIN.
Repeat.

I DON'T KNOW WHAT
RECEPTION I'M AT, BUT
FOR GOD'S SAKE
GIVE ME A GIN
AND TONIC.

DENIS THATCHER

NOW IS THE TIME

FOR DRINKING, NOW THE TIME TO DANCE FOOTLOOSE UPON THE EARTH.

HORACE

GIN AND MINT

**This bevvy is a summer favourite.
If you'd like a little more zing to it, add
a squeeze of lemon juice at the start.**

INGREDIENTS

50 ml gin · Two sprigs of fresh mint
Thin slice of cucumber · 100 ml elderflower
pressé · Cucumber or mint to garnish
Squeeze of lemon juice (optional)

METHOD

Stir together the gin, mint and cucumber
(and squeeze of lemon juice, if being
used) in a cocktail shaker, making sure
you bruise the mint and cucumber.

Strain into a cocktail glass and top
with the pressé. Garnish with a sprig
of mint or a slice of cucumber.

Sober or blotto, this is your motto: keep muddling through.

P. G. Wodehouse

WHAT HARM IN DRINKING CAN THERE BE, SINCE PUNCH AND LIFE SO WELL AGREE?

THOMAS BLACKLOCK

MAN, BEING REASONABLE, MUST GET DRUNK; THE BEST OF LIFE IS BUT INTOXICATION.

LORD BYRON

MEDIUM MARTINI

Harry Craddock was the head bartender at the Savoy's American Bar and is credited with popularising the Martini. This recipe, as well as over seven hundred others, is in his greatest work, *The Savoy Cocktail Book*.

INGREDIENTS

20 ml dry vermouth · 20 ml sweet vermouth
40 ml dry gin · Orange or lemon
twist to garnish

METHOD

Shake the vermouth and gin well in a cooled cocktail shaker and strain into a Martini glass. Serve with either a twist of lemon or orange.

A PERFECT MARTINI
SHOULD BE MADE
BY FILLING A
GLASS WITH GIN,
THEN WAVING IT
IN THE GENERAL
DIRECTION OF ITALY.

NOËL COWARD

RED MEAT
AND GIN.

JULIA CHILD ON THE
SECRET TO HER LONGEVITY

DRINK

IS THE FEAST OF REASON AND THE FLOW OF SOUL.

ALEXANDER POPE

ENGLISH GARDEN

This is a modern cocktail, reportedly invented in London in 2001, and is the result of a collaboration between bartenders Daniel Warner and Tobias Blazquez-Garcia.

INGREDIENTS

25 ml gin · 50 ml freshly squeezed apple juice · 20 ml freshly squeezed lime juice 20 ml sugar syrup · Sprig of mint · Slice of cucumber, plus extra to garnish

METHOD

Fill a cocktail shaker with ice and add the gin, apple juice, lime juice and syrup.

Bruise in the mint and cucumber and strain into a Collins glass. Serve with a slice of cucumber.

DRINK BECAUSE YOU
ARE HAPPY, BUT NEVER
BECAUSE YOU ARE
MISERABLE.

G. K. CHESTERTON

GIN ISN'T REALLY

A DRINK;
IT'S MORE A
MASCARA THINNER.

DYLAN MORAN

NINETY-NINE
PER CENT OF
ALL PROBLEMS
CAN BE SOLVED
BY MONEY – AND
FOR THE OTHER
ONE PER CENT
THERE'S ALCOHOL.

QUENTIN R. BUFOGLE

NEGRONI

The Negroni is reportedly named after the Italian Count Negroni. He asked for the Americano cocktail to be served with gin instead of soda water and the Negroni was born.

INGREDIENTS

30 ml gin · 30 ml Campari · 30 ml sweet vermouth · Orange peel to garnish

METHOD

Fill an Old-fashioned glass halfway to the brim with ice.

Pour the ingredients over the ice and stir. Garnish with the orange peel.

IT TAKES ONLY
ONE DRINK TO GET
ME DRUNK. THE
TROUBLE IS, I CAN'T
REMEMBER IF IT'S
THE THIRTEENTH OR
THE FOURTEENTH.

GEORGE BURNS

Home

IS
WHERE
THE
GIN IS.

Gin and drugs, dear lady, gin and drugs.

T. S. Eliot
on his inspiration

ABSTAINER: A WEAK PERSON WHO YIELDS TO THE TEMPTATION OF DENYING HIMSELF A PLEASURE.

AMBROSE BIERCE

FRENCH 75

Invented in Paris, the kick of the alcohol was said to have felt like being shelled by the French 75-mm field gun used in World War One.

INGREDIENTS

30 ml gin · 15 ml freshly squeezed lemon juice · 1 tsp icing sugar · Champagne to finish · Lemon twist to garnish

METHOD

Mix the gin, lemon juice and sugar together.

Pour into a champagne flute containing cracked ice and fill to the top with champagne. Garnish with a twist of lemon.

I FEEL
WONDERFUL
AND SAD.
IT'S THE GIN.

STEPHEN BERESFORD

DRINK
NOT THE
THIRD GLASS,
WHICH THOU
CANST NOT
TAME, WHEN
ONCE IT IS
WITHIN THEE.

GEORGE HERBERT

SIMPLY ENJOY
LIFE
AND THE GREAT
PLEASURES
THAT COME
WITH IT.

KAROLÍNA KURKOVÁ

TOM COLLINS

The first written instance of this classic cocktail appeared in 1876, in a book by famous American mixologist Jerry Thomas.

INGREDIENTS

45 ml gin · 30 ml freshly squeezed lemon juice · 15 ml sugar syrup · Soda water to finish · Lemon slice and maraschino cherry to garnish

METHOD

Fill a highball or Collins glass nearly to the brim with ice.

Mix the gin, lemon juice and sugar syrup together.

Top up with soda water and garnish with a slice of lemon and a maraschino cherry on a cocktail stick.

A MAN MUST DEFEND HIS
HOME, HIS WIFE, HIS
CHILDREN, AND
HIS MARTINI.

JACKIE GLEASON

TOO MUCH WORK

AND NO VACATION
**DESERVES
AT LEAST A**
SMALL LIBATION.

OSCAR WILDE

COME, LANDLORD,
FILL A FLOWING
BOWL UNTIL IT DOES
RUN OVER; TONIGHT
WE WILL ALL MERRY
BE – TOMORROW
WE'LL GET SOBER.

JOHN FLETCHER

PINK GIN

This classic cocktail features strongly in pop culture; even James Bond orders one, in the 1965 novel *The Man with the Golden Gun.*

INGREDIENTS

Three dashes bitters · 60 ml gin
Lemon twist to garnish

METHOD

Add the bitters to an Old-fashioned glass and swirl to coat the inside. Drain off any excess liquid.

Pour in the gin and garnish with a lemon twist.

ALCOHOL MAY
BE MAN'S WORST
ENEMY, BUT THE
BIBLE SAYS LOVE
YOUR ENEMY.

FRANK SINATRA

SOBRIETY DIMINISHES, DISCRIMINATES AND SAYS NO; DRUNKENNESS EXPANDS, UNITES AND SAYS YES.

WILLIAM JAMES

WHEN A
MAN WHO IS
DRINKING NEAT
GIN STARTS
TALKING ABOUT
HIS MOTHER
HE IS PAST ALL
ARGUMENT.

C. S. FORESTER

BEE'S KNEES

The rumour is that this Prohibition-era cocktail was flavoured with lemon and honey to hide the taste of the bathtub gin it was made with!

INGREDIENTS

50 ml gin · 10 ml runny honey · 1 tsp water
15 ml freshly squeezed lemon juice
Lemon twist to garnish

METHOD

Stir the honey into the water until blended.

Pour into a cooled cocktail glass
and mix in the gin and lemon juice.
Serve with a lemon twist.

No poems can please
for long or live that are
written by water-drinkers.

Horace

DON'T
COME IN
IF YOU
DIDN'T
BRING
gin.

TEETOTALLERS LACK THE SYMPATHY AND GENEROSITY OF MEN THAT DRINK.

W. H. DAVIES

NO ANIMAL EVER INVENTED
ANYTHING SO BAD AS
DRUNKENNESS – OR
SO GOOD AS
DRINK.

G. K. CHESTERTON

SINGAPORE SLING

The Singapore Sling was famously invented at Raffles Hotel in Singapore.

INGREDIENTS

30 ml gin · 15 ml cherry liqueur
7.5 ml Cointreau · 7.5 ml DOM Bénédictine
10 ml grenadine · 120 ml freshly squeezed
pineapple juice · 15 ml freshly squeezed
lime juice · Dash Angostura bitters
Lemon slice and maraschino
cherry to garnish

METHOD

Add the ingredients to a cocktail shaker full
of ice cubes. Shake and strain into a Sling
glass and serve with a slice of lemon and
a maraschino cherry on a cocktail stick.

I WOULD LIKE
TO OBSERVE THE
VERMOUTH FROM
ACROSS THE ROOM
WHILE I DRINK
MY MARTINI.

WINSTON CHURCHILL

THE DRINK YOU

LIKE THE BEST
SHOULD BE THE
DRINK YOU DRINK
THE MOST.

J. B. BURGESS

A drink a day keeps the shrink away.

Edward Abbey

VESPER

Ian Fleming invented the Vesper, introducing it in the 1953 James Bond novel *Casino Royale*. Bond named it after the beautiful Vesper Lynd.

INGREDIENTS

60 ml gin · 20 ml vodka · 10 ml Lillet Blanc or Cocchi Americano · Thin strip of lemon

METHOD

Shake the liquid ingredients together with ice in a shaker and strain into a Martini glass. Serve with the lemon.

I NEVER
GO JOGGING;
IT MAKES ME
SPILL MY MARTINI.

GEORGE BURNS

DRINKING
IS A WAY
OF ENDING
THE DAY.

ERNEST HEMINGWAY

WHEN I DRINK, I
THINK; AND WHEN
I THINK, I DRINK.

FRANÇOIS RABELAIS

THE CHURCH
IS NEAR, BUT
THE ROAD IS
ICY. THE BAR
IS FAR, BUT
I WILL WALK
CAREFULLY.

RUSSIAN PROVERB

LONG ISLAND ICE TEA

This drink's origins are hotly contested; many claim it was invented by Old Man Bishop during the Prohibition era.

INGREDIENTS

15 ml vodka • 15 ml gin • 15 ml white rum 15 ml tequila • 15 ml triple sec • 30 ml freshly squeezed lemon juice • 30 ml gomme syrup • Splash cola • Lemon twist or wedge to garnish

METHOD

Fill a highball glass halfway to the brim with ice.

Pour the ingredients over and stir. Serve with a twist or wedge of lemon.

A MAN'S GOT TO
BELIEVE
IN SOMETHING.
I BELIEVE
I'LL HAVE
ANOTHER
DRINK.

W. C. FIELDS

THE PROPER
UNION OF GIN
AND VERMOUTH
IS A GREAT AND
SUDDEN GLORY;
IT IS ONE OF
THE HAPPIEST
MARRIAGES ON
EARTH, AND
ONE OF THE
SHORTEST LIVED.

BERNARD DeVOTO

KEEPING ONE'S GUESTS
SUPPLIED WITH LIQUOR
IS THE FIRST LAW OF
HOSPITALITY.

MARGARET WAY

PINK LADY

This cocktail is said to have been a favourite of pink-fanatic screen siren Jayne Mansfield, who reportedly drank one before every meal.

INGREDIENTS

45 ml gin · One egg white · Four dashes grenadine · Maraschino cherry to garnish

METHOD

Fill a cocktail shaker with ice and shake together the ingredients.

Strain into a cocktail glass and serve with maraschino cherry.

WOMAN FIRST

TEMPTED MAN
TO EAT; HE TOOK TO
DRINKING OF HIS
OWN ACCORD.

JOHN R.
KEMBLE

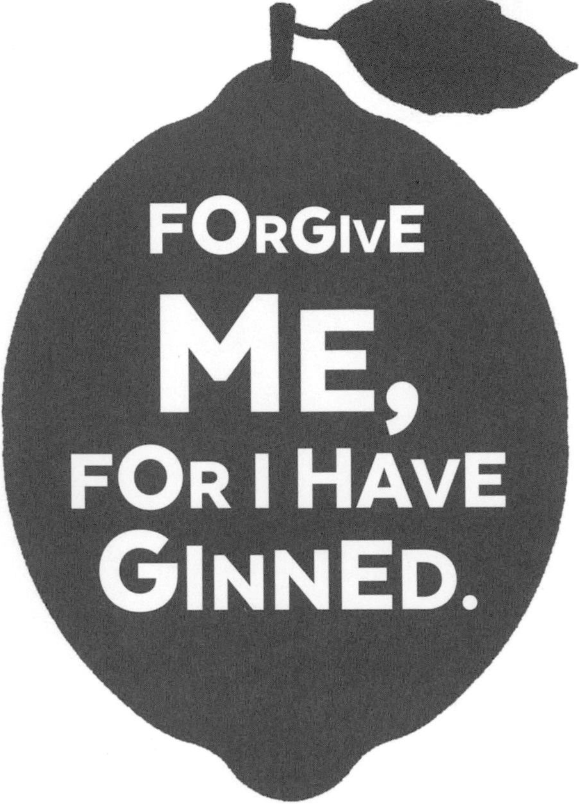
FORGIVE
ME,
FOR I HAVE
GINNED.

Reality is an illusion created by a lack of alcohol.

N. F. Simpson

BUT I'M NOT SO THINK AS YOU DRUNK I AM.

J. C. SQUIRE

DRY MARTINI

Writer Ernest Hemingway preferred a 'Montgomery' dry Martini – 15 parts gin to one part vermouth. This recipe isn't quite so potent.

INGREDIENTS

30 ml dry vermouth · 60 ml dry gin
Dash orange bitters · Orange or lemon twist to garnish

METHOD

Shake well in a cooled cocktail shaker and strain into a Martini glass. Serve with a twist of orange or lemon.

A MAN OUGHT TO
GET DRUNK AT
LEAST TWICE A
YEAR... SO HE WON'T
LET HIMSELF GET
SNOTTY ABOUT IT.

RAYMOND CHANDLER

THE PROBLEM WITH
THE WORLD IS THAT
EVERYONE IS A FEW
DRINKS BEHIND.

HUMPHREY BOGART

WHEN I'M DRUNK, I BITE.

I BITE.

BETTE MIDLER

GIN AND TONIC

Which garnish you use will depend on
the flavour you are trying to enhance:
for dry gin, try lime or an olive; for
floral gins, try grapefruit, rosemary
or cucumber; for citrusy or spiced
gins, add coriander or orange.

INGREDIENTS

30 ml gin · 90 ml tonic
Suitable garnish

METHOD

Put several ice cubes into a highball or Copa
de Balon glass and pour the ingredients
over. Serve with appropriate garnish.

WHAT'S DRINKING?
A MERE PAUSE
FROM
THINKING!

LORD BYRON

TURN
IMPOSSIBLE
INTO
GIN
possible!

BELOVED, WE
JOIN HANDS
HERE TO PRAY
FOR GIN...
OUR INNARDS
THIRST FOR
THE JUICE OF
JUNIPER.

WALLACE THURMAN

HERE'S TO

ALCOHOL, THE
ROSE-COLOURED
GLASSES
OF LIFE.

F. SCOTT
FITZGERALD

THE LAST WORD

When The Last Word first appeared on the Detroit Athletic Club's menu in 1916, it cost 35 cents and was the club's most expensive drink.

INGREDIENTS

30 ml gin · 20 ml green chartreuse
20 ml maraschino liqueur · 20 ml freshly squeezed lime juice · Lime wedge or maraschino cherry to garnish

METHOD

Fill a cocktail shaker with ice and add the ingredients. Add a splash of chilled water to taste if necessary.

Shake together then strain into a Martini or coupe glass. Serve with a wedge of lime or a maraschino cherry.

I had never tasted anything so cool and clean.

Ernest Hemingway
on Martinis

YOU'RE NOT DRUNK IF YOU CAN LIE ON THE FLOOR WITHOUT HOLDING ON.

DEAN MARTIN

HAPPINESS IS...
FINDING TWO
OLIVES IN YOUR
MARTINI WHEN
YOU'RE HUNGRY.

JOHNNY CARSON

PEGU CLUB

This cocktail was the signature drink of Burma's Pegu Club, the social centre for colonial Britons in the 1920s.

INGREDIENTS

60 ml gin · 30 ml orange liqueur
20 ml freshly squeezed lime juice
Dash orange bitters · Slice of lime

METHOD

Combine all the liquid ingredients in a shaker, add ice and shake well.

Strain into a cocktail glass and serve with a slice of lime.

NOTHING IS
MORE PLEASURABLE
THAN TO SIT IN
THE SHADE, SIP GIN
AND CONTEMPLATE
OTHER PEOPLE'S
ADULTERIES.

JOHN SKOW

SOMETIMES
TOO MUCH TO
DRINK
IS BARELY
ENOUGH.

MARK TWAIN

I DRINK WHEN I HAVE
OCCASION, AND
SOMETIMES WHEN
I HAVE NO
OCCASION.

MIGUEL DE CERVANTES

CLOVER CLUB

The Clover Club is named
after a nineteenth-century
Philadelphia men's club.

INGREDIENTS

40 ml gin · 10 ml sweet vermouth
Handful fresh raspberries · 10 ml freshly
squeezed lemon juice · 2 tsp raspberry syrup
One egg white · Lemon twist
or raspberry to garnish

METHOD

Combine and shake all the ingredients
vigorously for 10 seconds, then add ice
and shake for another 10 seconds.

Strain into a cocktail or coupe glass and
serve with a lemon twist or a raspberry.

NEVER TRUST A

MAN WHO
DOESN'T
DRINK.

JAMES
CRUMLEY

THE THREE-
MARTINI LUNCH
IS THE EPITOME
OF AMERICAN
EFFICIENCY. WHERE
ELSE CAN YOU
GET AN EARFUL,
A BELLYFUL AND
A SNOOTFUL AT
THE SAME TIME?

GERALD FORD

The worse you are
at thinking, the better
you are at drinking.

Terry Goodkind

GIBSON

The Gibson featured in Hitchcock's *North by Northwest* when Cary Grant's impeccably dressed Roger Thornhill orders one during a seductive dinner on a train.

INGREDIENTS

70 ml gin · Dash dry vermouth
Two cocktail onions to garnish

METHOD

Pour the ingredients into an ice-filled shaker and stir for 5–10 seconds.

Strain into a Martini glass and garnish with two cocktail onions.

I AM PREPARED
TO BELIEVE THAT
A DRY MARTINI
SLIGHTLY IMPAIRS
THE PALATE, BUT
THINK WHAT IT DOES
FOR THE SOUL.

ALEC WAUGH

IT'S
NEVER
TOO
EARLY
FOR
gin
o'clock.

I HAVE TAKEN
MORE OUT
OF ALCOHOL
THAN ALCOHOL
HAS TAKEN
OUT OF ME.

WINSTON CHURCHILL

DRINK
WHAT YOU WANT;
DRINK
WHAT YOU'RE ABLE.
IF YOU ARE DRINKING
WITH ME,
YOU'LL BE
UNDER THE
TABLE.

ANONYMOUS

THE MOLL

The Moll is named after writer Daniel Defoe's enterprising heroine, Moll Flanders.

INGREDIENTS

30 ml sloe gin · 30 ml gin · 30 ml dry vermouth · Dash orange bitters
1 tsp sugar or sugar syrup

METHOD

Shake the ingredients over ice in a shaker.
Strain into a chilled cocktail glass.

AH, DRINK AGAIN THIS RIVER
THAT IS THE TAKER-AWAY
OF PAIN AND THE
GIVER-BACK OF
BEAUTY!

EDNA ST VINCENT MILLAY

HE WAS

WHITE AND
SHAKEN, LIKE A
DRY MARTINI.

P. G. WODEHOUSE

ALWAYS DO SOBER
WHAT YOU SAID
YOU'D DO DRUNK.
THAT WILL TEACH
YOU TO KEEP YOUR
MOUTH SHUT.

ERNEST HEMINGWAY

RIVIERA SNOB

The aperitif Aperol was invented by
the Barbieri brothers in 1919 and
marketed specifically at women
because of its low alcohol content.

INGREDIENTS

60 ml Aperol · 30 ml gin · 20 ml freshly
squeezed lemon juice · 15 ml sugar syrup
Soda water to finish · Orange peel to garnish

METHOD

Combine ingredients in a chilled cocktail
shaker and shake well until cooled.

Strain into a coupe glass, top up
with soda water and garnish
with a twist of orange peel.

MARTINIS

ARE THE ONLY
**AMERICAN
INVENTION**
AS PERFECT AS
THE SONNET.

H. L. MENCKEN

HEALTH – WHAT MY FRIENDS
ARE ALWAYS DRINKING
TO BEFORE THEY
FALL DOWN.

PHYLLIS DILLER

YOU HAVE TO

DRINK. OTHERWISE
YOU'D GO STARK
STARING
SOBER.

KEITH
WATERHOUSE

LAVENDER AND GIN

The lavender taste gives a traditional English summertime feel to this cocktail.

INGREDIENTS

50 ml lavender gin (see below)
100 ml lemonade · Freshly squeezed lemon
juice · Lavender stalk to garnish

METHOD

To make the lavender gin, add
20 dried lavender flower heads to a
70 cl bottle of gin and leave overnight
to infuse, then remove the lavender.

Add the gin to an ice-filled highball
glass and top up with the lemonade.
Add a dash of lemon juice and stir.

Garnish with a lavender stalk.

TIME IS NEVER
WASTED
WHEN YOU'RE
WASTED ALL
THE TIME.

CATHERINE ZANDONELLA

Drunkenness is nothing
but voluntary madness.

Seneca the Younger

I FEAR THE MAN
WHO DRINKS WATER
AND SO REMEMBERS
THIS MORNING WHAT
THE REST OF US
SAID LAST NIGHT.

ANONYMOUS

MONKEY GLAND

This cocktail is named after the unsavoury historical practice of grafting a monkey testicle to a human in the belief that it would make one live longer.

INGREDIENTS

60 ml gin · 40 ml freshly squeezed orange juice · 1 tsp grenadine · 1 tsp sugar syrup 1 tsp absinthe · Orange twist to garnish

METHOD

Put the ingredients into a shaker with ice and shake well.

Strain into a cocktail glass and garnish with a twist of orange.

A MAN CAN HIDE
ALL THINGS,
EXCEPTING TWAIN
- THAT HE IS
DRUNK, AND THAT
HE IS IN LOVE.

ANTIPHANES

GIN MAKES THE WORLD GO ROUND.

I NEVER
MET A PUB
I DIDN'T
LIKE.

PETE SLOSBERG

ALCOHOL
MAY NOT SOLVE
YOUR
PROBLEMS,
BUT NEITHER
WILL WATER
OR MILK.

ANONYMOUS

LONDON FOG

The cocktail gained this name thanks to its murky green colour: it is a similar hue to the 'pea-soup' fog that pervaded London until the twentieth century.

INGREDIENTS

40 ml gin · 20 ml Pernod
Orange twist to garnish

METHOD

Fill an Old-fashioned glass with crushed ice and add the ingredients.

Stir well, adding more ice if necessary and an orange twist to garnish.

I ENVY PEOPLE WHO DRINK
– AT LEAST THEY KNOW
WHAT TO BLAME
EVERYTHING
ON.

OSCAR LEVANT

THE DRUNK MIND

SPEAKS
THE SOBER
HEART.

ANONYMOUS

I NEVER DRINK
WHILE I'M
WORKING, BUT
AFTER A FEW
GLASSES I GET
IDEAS THAT WOULD
NEVER HAVE
OCCURRED TO
ME DEAD SOBER.

IRWIN SHAW

CAMOMILE AND GIN

Camomile is said to have many health benefits: it can be used to treat anything from hay fever to chicken pox!

INGREDIENTS

60 ml gin · 25 ml camomile tea
25 ml freshly squeezed pink grapefruit
or lemon juice · 15 ml honey
Lime twist to garnish

METHOD

Shake the ingredients vigorously
in a shaker until mixed.

Strain into a coupe glass and
garnish with a twist of lime.

I drink exactly
as much as I want,
and one drink more.

H. L. Mencken

ALCOHOL IS A MISUNDERSTOOD VITAMIN.

P. G. WODEHOUSE

I HAVE A THEORY
THAT THE SECRET
OF MARITAL
HAPPINESS IS
SIMPLE: DRINK
IN DIFFERENT
PUBS TO YOUR
OTHER HALF.

JILLY COOPER

AVIATION

If the crème de violette proves difficult to find, a variation in *The Savoy Cocktail Book* allows it to be omitted, although the drink will lose its distinctive lavender colour.

INGREDIENTS

60 ml gin • 15 ml maraschino liqueur
10 ml crème de violette • 20 ml freshly squeezed lemon juice • Cherry or lemon twist to garnish

METHOD

Combine all the liquid ingredients in a shaker, add ice and shake well until mixed.

Strain into a chilled cocktail glass and serve with a cherry or a twist of lemon.

THE ONLY CURE FOR A REAL HANGOVER IS DEATH.

ROBERT BENCHLEY

HOW MUCH OF
OUR LITERATURE,
OUR POLITICAL LIFE,
OUR FRIENDSHIPS
AND LOVE AFFAIRS,
DEPEND ON BEING
ABLE TO TALK
PEACEFULLY
IN A BAR!

JOHN WAIN

ALCOHOL IS LIKE LOVE. THE FIRST KISS IS MAGIC, THE SECOND IS INTIMATE, THE THIRD IS ROUTINE.

RAYMOND CHANDLER

OLD ETONIAN

The Old Etonian takes its name from Eton College and enjoyed its heyday in the mid 1920s, when it was quaffed around London.

INGREDIENTS

40 ml gin · 40 ml Lillet Blanc or Cocchi Americano · Dash crème de noyaux · Dash orange bitters Orange twist to garnish

METHOD

Add the ingredients to a shaker filled with ice and shake.

Strain into a cocktail glass and garnish with a twist of orange.

ALCOHOL IS THE
ANAESTHESIA BY WHICH
WE ENDURE THE
OPERATION
OF LIFE.

GEORGE BERNARD SHAW

THERE IS
NOTHING WHICH
HAS YET BEEN
CONTRIVED BY
MAN, BY WHICH SO
MUCH HAPPINESS
IS PRODUCED
AS BY A GOOD
TAVERN OR INN.

SAMUEL JOHNSON

Tea is so tame.
A cocktail is lots
more naughty.

Richard Florance

SLOE GIN FIZZ

Sloe gin is so popular in the UK that there are several competitions and awards, including the Sloe Gin World Championships in East Sussex.

INGREDIENTS

60 ml sloe gin · 30 ml freshly squeezed lemon or lime juice
1 tsp sugar syrup · 115 ml soda water
Slice of lemon to garnish

METHOD

Shake the gin, lemon or lime juice and sugar syrup over ice in a shaker.

Strain into an ice-filled highball or Sling glass. Top up with the soda water and stir. Garnish with a slice of lemon.

ALCOHOL IS
NECESSARY FOR
A MAN SO THAT
HE CAN HAVE A
GOOD OPINION
OF HIMSELF,
UNDISTURBED
BY THE FACTS.

FINLEY PETER DUNNE

BACCHUS:
A CONVENIENT DEITY INVENTED BY THE ANCIENTS AS AN EXCUSE FOR GETTING DRUNK.

AMBROSE BIERCE

THE WORST THING
ABOUT SOME MEN
IS THAT WHEN THEY
ARE NOT DRUNK
THEY ARE SOBER.

W. B. YEATS

FIFTY-FIFTY MARTINI

Also known as a 'Perfect Martini', it is possible that this is the original recipe for the Martini before it evolved into the more bracing drink of today.

INGREDIENTS

40 ml gin · 40 ml dry vermouth
Two dashes orange bitters (optional)
Olive to garnish

METHOD

Combine the ingredients and ice in a shaker and stir for 20 seconds.

Strain into a Martini glass and garnish with an olive.

THE GIN AND
TONIC HAS
SAVED MORE
ENGLISHMEN'S
LIVES, AND
MINDS, THAN
ALL THE
DOCTORS IN
THE EMPIRE.

WINSTON CHURCHILL

DRINK
THE FIRST.
SIP THE SECOND
SLOWLY.
SKIP THE
THIRD.

KNUTE ROCKNE

MY GRANDMOTHER IS OVER
80 AND STILL DOESN'T
NEED GLASSES. DRINKS
RIGHT OUT OF
THE BOTTLE.

HENNY YOUNGMAN

MAE ROSE

You'll need to stir this cocktail
a little longer than usual as it
should be served very cold.

INGREDIENTS
40 ml gin · 20 ml dry vermouth
12.5 ml Campari · 12.5 ml grapefruit liqueur
Grapefruit twist to garnish

METHOD
Put the ingredients and ice into a shaker and
stir until the shaker is cold on the outside.

Strain into a coupe glass and serve
with a twist of grapefruit.

ONE MORE DRINK

AND I'D HAVE
BEEN UNDER
THE HOST.

DOROTHY
PARKER

If you're interested in finding out more about our books, find us on Facebook at **Summersdale Publishers** and follow us on Twitter at **@Summersdale**.

www.summersdale.com

Image credits

pp.1, 9, 21, 32, 47, 63, 70, 83, 95, 106, 123, 135, 147 – Copa de Balon glass © tovovan/Shutterstock.com
pp.3, 19, 37, 55, 82, 100, 127, 145, 159 – lemon © BATKA/Shutterstock.com; leaf © Daria Voskoboeva/Shutterstock.com
pp.4, 14, 18, 27, 30, 36, 42, 50, 56, 59, 69, 74, 81, 86, 93, 99, 104, 114, 115, 120, 126, 132, 138, 142, 149, 158 – lemon slice © Kate Cooper
pp.5, 6–7, 10–11, 23, 34, 48, 60, 73, 84, 96, 108, 124, 137, 150, 160 – stripy pattern © Kate Cooper
p.10 – juniper berries © Kate Cooper
pp.13, 16, 29, 41, 54, 66, 79, 90, 102, 113, 119, 131, 144, 156 – cocktail glass © Creative icon styles/Shutterstock.com
pp.18, 30, 42, 56, 69, 81, 93, 104, 114, 120, 132, 142, 158 – bottle © Chloe Platt/Shutterstock.com
pp.28, 46, 64, 91, 109, 118, 136, 154 – cocktail shaker © Sergey Mastepanov/Shutterstock.com